King Fernando

John Bartholomew
Illustrated by Susie Jenkin-Pearce

A & C Black · London

The Comets Series

Series Editor, Amy Gibbs

King Fernando	John Bartholomew
A Witch in Time	Terry Deary
Tom's Sausage Lion	Michael Morpurgo
Odin's Monster	Susan Price
The Air-Raid Shelter	Jeremy Strong

Bartholomew, John
King Fernando. (Comets)
I. Title II. Series
823'.914[J] PZ7

ISBN 0-7136-2733-6

Published by A & C Black (Publishers) Limited
35 Bedford Row, London WC1R 4JH

First published 1986

ISBN 0-7136-2733-6

Filmset by August Filmsetting, Haydock, St Helens
Printed by R J Acford, Chichester, Sussex

I

King Fernando

Even from a mile away, you always knew when King Fernando was coming. There was a fanfare from the horn, on every bend. Louder and louder, the horn blasts would approach. After a while, the King would sweep majestically round the last corner, and screech to a stop by the waiting people.

Five times a day, King Fernando made the journey into town from the villages in the hills; and five times a day crawled back up the steep road for the return journey. King Fernando was red, apart from a blue stripe just below its windows, a painting of a grinning head wearing a crown on its front radiator, and crookedly lettered signs on its sides, which read:

THE KING FERNANDO BUS COMPANY

Calvin heard the long horn blast as he came out of his yard, and knew the bus would arrive in a few minutes. He was carrying a large basket full of eggs, each one carefully wrapped in a piece of Gleaner paper. His mother sold eggs and oranges every Saturday in the city market. She would go down and set up her stall on Friday, and it was Calvin's job to bring her fresh eggs the next morning after collecting them from seven or eight of their neighbours who kept fowl.

A large crowd, mostly women and children, waited outside the post office where the bus would stop. Their baskets were mostly empty. Saturday was a buying day at the market. Most of the goods to be sold had been carried down the day before, by people like Calvin's mother. On Fridays, the roof-rack of the bus was always piled high with bunches of bananas and sacks of yams.

When the bus stopped, everybody pressed forward. They were all eager to be first on, to try to get the few remaining seats. Being small, Calvin managed to worm his way through to the doorway quite quickly. He pretended not to hear the fat lady behind him who grumbled about 'pickneys borin' in', and he got his foot onto the step of the bus. He clutched his basket protectively.

'No room to put that in the bus!' said the conductress, looking at his bulky basket. 'Mus' go'pon the roof.'

'Is heggs, man,' protested Calvin, 'Dem mash up 'pon the roof.'

The conductress sniffed, but allowed him to bring the basket on without further objection. Calvin handed her the twenty-five cents fare and made his way to one of the back seats. He managed to put his basket underneath it safely and even to squeeze himself into a narrow space between two other people. He wasn't allowed to stay there for long, however. The lady who had been behind him in the queue, made her way down the bus, jerked her head at Calvin, and said 'Get up from there. Me 'avin' that seat.'

Calvin gave up the seat willingly enough, but he wished she had asked him a bit more politely. He smiled secretly to himself as he watched her trying to budge up the tightly packed people on either side of her, and settle herself comfortably in the tiny opening. Really, she would have been better off standing. For a second, she saw him grinning. She looked hard at him, but said nothing.

By the time the bus moved away, there were several people standing. There was a tremendous jerk as the driver let in the clutch, and the ancient bus heaved itself into motion. Calvin swayed against the lady who had taken his seat, banging her legs and nearly falling onto her lap.

'Ftch!' she muttered, clicking her tongue behind her teeth. 'Cho!'

Most of the passengers were chattering cheerfully. Market day was a great day for gossip. It was hot and stuffy, and people pressed so tightly against Calvin that he couldn't move, but he didn't mind. It was the same every week and he hardly noticed.

The driver went fast and cool air breezed in through the open windows. Quite a lot of them had no glass anyway, and were never closed even when it was raining. The driver calmly tore into sharp hairpin bends; he had one hand on the wheel and one pulling the hanging string which sounded the horn almost continuously. Frightening glimpses of steep drops from the unfenced edges of the roads flashed past. The wheels bounced in and out of potholes and the whole bus shook and rattled. It was a miracle that it didn't fall to pieces. Calvin watched the road rushing underneath him through a gap in the wooden floorboards.

No one ever got in the way. People heard King Fernando coming a long way off, and everyone moved off the road before it reached them.

The bus stopped at Limegrove. It seemed impossible that anyone else could possibly squeeze in, but everyone shuffled up.

Three youths, about seventeen years old, got on. They spoke loudly, and roughly pushed their way past people. They were all laughing. In spite of the crush, passengers made way for them to get

through, and one of them plumped himself down onto a seat which was already full. The old man who was sitting there had to shove up quickly against his neighbour to avoid being sat on. The second one carried a huge radio cassette player, tuned in very loudly to RJR Radio Jamaica. The third boy ended up next to Calvin, nearly treading on his feet. The passengers closest to these louts fell silent, their mouths set in straight lines of disapproval. Those further away muttered about their behaviour. The happy mood within the bus disappeared.

As the bus swept on down the hill towards the town, Calvin, still pinned to the spot by the crush of

people around him, felt a stealthy movement against his shoulder. The youth next to him was gently moving his hand down, his eyes concentrating on the back trouser pocket of a man who stood near them. The man had deliberately turned his back on the unwelcome company. A folded wad of money showed over the top of his pocket, a small strip of green.

Calvin realised with a shock that the youth was about to pick the man's pocket. He broke out into a sweat. There was so much fidgeting and shifting between the passengers that a pick-pocket could do his work easily. Calvin had heard how they did it. One would carefully lift out the goods and pass it to a companion. By the time its loss was discovered, it would have been passed again to someone else some distance away, whom no one would suspect. There might even be a fourth accomplice in the bus, one who couldn't be connected with the youths.

Calvin couldn't say anything. The deed had not yet been done, he would look a fool. If he waited, the money would have been passed on by the time he told anybody. He watched the gently moving hand in horrified fascination.

The bus lurched round another bend, and Calvin stumbled against the youth. For a moment, their eyes met, the youth looking angrily at Calvin as if it was his fault. Without even thinking about what he was doing, Calvin slowly lowered his eyes towards the man's pocket, and stared fixedly at the protruding cash. The youth knew he was watching, and his hand stopped moving. For some minutes, Calvin never took his eyes off the pocket. Then he looked up. He found two eyes staring at him, narrow slits, full of hate.

He didn't like that look, he didn't like the thought of what the youth might do to him, but, for the moment, he felt strangely calm. Nothing was going to happen in this crowd and if he kept watching, the money would be all right.

The bus stopped at Ardgarten, and a few passengers got in.

'We gettin' off 'ere,' said the youth abruptly to his companions.

'Eh?' said the one with the radio, 'But we goin' to . . .'

'We gettin' off,' he repeated.

The conductress closed the door, and the engine revved.

'Hold it, driver, we gettin' off,' called the youth, and the conductress grumbled as she opened the door again.

Even then, the youth didn't move. He faced Calvin, his eyes small as a snake's, and he hissed, half in venom, half in admiration, 'Cool, man.'

Then they were off, the three of them, barging their way down to the door, not caring one bit who they trampled on or shoved. A girl about their age got off at the same time.

The door closed behind them, and it was as if everybody came back to life. The cheerful chatter resumed, the old man spread himself back more comfortably over his seat, and Calvin himself relaxed after the tension of the last few minutes.

'Hey, Mister,' he said, 'Your money nearly fallin' out, you know. Y'll lose it.'

'Oh . . . t'anks,' said the man, casually thrusting it deeper into his pocket.

If only he knew.

2

Where is the Driver?

Most of the seats in the bus were made from wooden slats. The one exception was the driver's seat. This had once been rather grand, and even now, though the leather was cracked and worn and hairy bits of coarse stuffing were escaping from it, it was still, without doubt, the most comfortable seat King Fernando had. After all, the driver did have to sit in it all day long.

On the driver's left was the engine. It was completely inside the bus and most of its metal casing was now missing. Passengers had to take care not to fall into it when the bus jerked, and conversation was impossible anywhere near it, because of the noise. On uphill runs especially, the moving metal parts would grind and squeal sickeningly.

Joe, the driver, was not really a tall man but he always wore a tall hat. Calvin had never seen him without it. He drove fast, and fiercely, and often needed a heavy touch on the brake as the bus hurtled into a bend, or if a careless goat was slow to get out of the way. Occasionally, when someone he knew got on, he might flash them a brief smile but usually he never smiled and never spoke.

The bus tore on down the hill, and shuddered to a stop at Redmount, the last district before it reached town. A handful of people got on there, squeezing in somehow. Joe the driver got out, swinging down to the ground through his own small door. Stooping slightly because his sitting position had made him stiff, he hurried across the road and entered a house without knocking.

When all the passengers were in, the conductress pressed the push button which worked a little light in front of the driver's seat – a bell would never have been heard amongst all the other noise.

It was only then that she realised that Joe was not there. Nobody minded. They had the whole day in front of them. The conductress shrugged her shoulders and chatted to the people nearby. The engine ticked over reassuringly. He would soon be back.

The few moments became several minutes. The easy-going chat of the passengers became a little irritable. Why was Joe taking so long? Everyone started to peer out of the window, towards the house, and a small child said loudly 'Why we stop?'

Several more minutes passed, and the front door of the house remained firmly closed. The engine was getting hot. Its rhythm changed and quite suddenly it stopped, sending a little shiver through the bus. Still Joe did not reappear.

People started to mutter.

'Where 'im garn?'

''As somten 'appen to 'im? Is 'e a'right?'

'Me gettin' very late, you know,' remarked the fat lady who had got on with Calvin. It didn't seem to occur to her that if she was getting late, then so was everybody else.

''im usually on'ee one or two minute.'

'Per'aps 'im 'urt 'imself.'

'Maybe 'e 'as a girlfrien' in there.' There was some laughter at this suggestion.

The conductress started to climb down, to go and see what was the matter. Then she changed her mind, thinking that she ought not to leave the bus. Her eye lighted on Calvin, who, by this time, was standing fairly close to her.

'Go in the 'ouse and find Joe,' she requested.

It seemed a small enough thing to do, but Calvin felt shy. He didn't know Joe at all, except by sight. He had ridden on King Fernando dozens of times, but had never spoken to Joe. He didn't know who lived in the house, and wasn't sure what to say. Maybe it was Joe's own house, and he had just

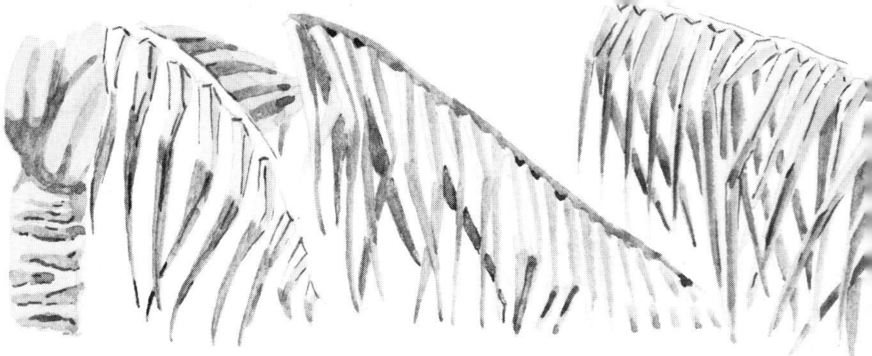

stopped to make a cool drink. Maybe he would be annoyed at being fetched. Calvin climbed down from the bus and walked slowly over to the house.

As he got nearer, he could hear the sound of a child crying loudly inside. The crying never stopped, it was more like screaming. The more Calvin heard of it, the less he liked it. What could be happening?

Nervously, he paused at the door.

‘’allo, anybody there?’

Well, that was silly, he thought to himself, I know there’s someone there. He tried again, a little louder.

‘’allo, there. ’allo!’

There was no reply. Calvin turned towards the bus. ‘Now what?’ The conductress flapped her hand at him from the doorway. ‘Go inside, go inside,’ she was saying.

Reluctantly, Calvin turned back and opened the door. There was no one to be seen in the cool darkness, but the screaming of the child could be heard clearly through the kitchen door, and Calvin went in.

A little girl of about six years old, was lying on her back on the floor, screaming and struggling, and Joe seemed to be trying to hold her down. A saucepan was on the floor near her. The floor was wet, and steam was rising.

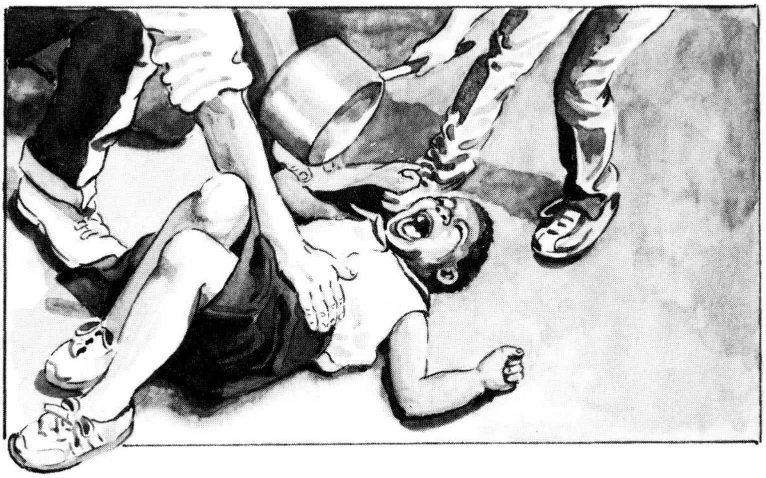

Joe looked round when Calvin came in, glad to see him.

'She try to take the boilin' water off the gas,' he explained briefly. 'All scald up.'

At the sight of a stranger, the little girl started to scream louder than ever. Calvin could see an awful puffy weal on her arm, stretching from her shoulder to her elbow. He clutched at his own arm for a second, as if he could feel the pain himself. The child was thrashing about, trying to find some comfort, and Joe held her still as firmly as he could, taking care to keep the injured arm off the tiled floor.

'Get some cold water,' he commanded.

Calvin went over to the sink and turned the tap on, but no water came out. Pipes were often dry in the uphill districts.

'Me look outside,' he said to Joe, and went out through the back door into the yard, carrying the empty pan. There, as he had hoped, was an oil drum with a pipe that led rain-water off the roof. He removed the piece of wood that covered it, and peered in. There was a little water at the bottom, but he couldn't reach it. He found a log, and rolled it up to the drum. Standing on the log and bending over the rim, he could just get the pan into the water. He swished it around for a moment to cool the metal which was still hot.

''orry 'op!' came Joe's voice from inside.

Calvin hurried in with the pan of cool water. Joe turned the little girl onto her side and held her arm so that the wound was uppermost.

'Pour the cold water on there.'

The little girl screamed louder than ever when she saw the pan of water.

'It cool, it cool,' said Joe reassuringly. 'Pour it genckle, man.'

So Calvin gently trickled the cool water on to her flesh. The child flinched, but as the water eased the burning and some of the pain left her face, she relaxed a little, stopped struggling with Joe, and became more still.

'We must tek 'er to harspital,' said Joe. 'Find somten to cover 'er harm.'

Calvin couldn't find a large enough cloth, but came back with a T-shirt and cotton dress which he discovered hanging up to dry. Joe chose the dress, and wrapped it loosely around her arm.

'That too fluffy,' he said, pointing to the T-shirt. 'Might stick to 'er harm – mek it worse when they tek it off.'

The house door opened and in came the girl's mother. She dropped the basket she was carrying with a shriek, and rushed across to the child. 'Wh'appen, Chereme?' she asked, and Joe stopped her just in time from squeezing the bad arm as she picked her up. Chereme had actually stopped crying for a moment when the scald was dressed, but now started again louder than ever as she clung to her mother.

'Oh Lord, me only go hout for a moment,' said the mother, first kissing Chereme, and then shouting at her 'Why you touch the pan?'

'Bring 'er out,' said Joe. 'We must go to the harspital.'

Calvin had forgotten the bus. Between them, they carried Chereme over and somehow, the passengers cleared a seat for her and her mother. Joe took a starting handle from under his seat, and jerked the engine back into life.

Down the hill roared King Fernando, past the closer packed houses as it came into town, round the courthouse square, and turned left towards the hospital instead of right towards the market.

They swept in at the hospital gate and Joe jumped from his seat to help Chereme and her mother inside.

'Hey, me garn be real late, you know,' said the fat lady crossly to him as he climbed back in. Everyone looked at her scornfully. Joe pretended not to hear. He started the bus without answering and drove it carefully through the city streets to the market. At last they arrived.

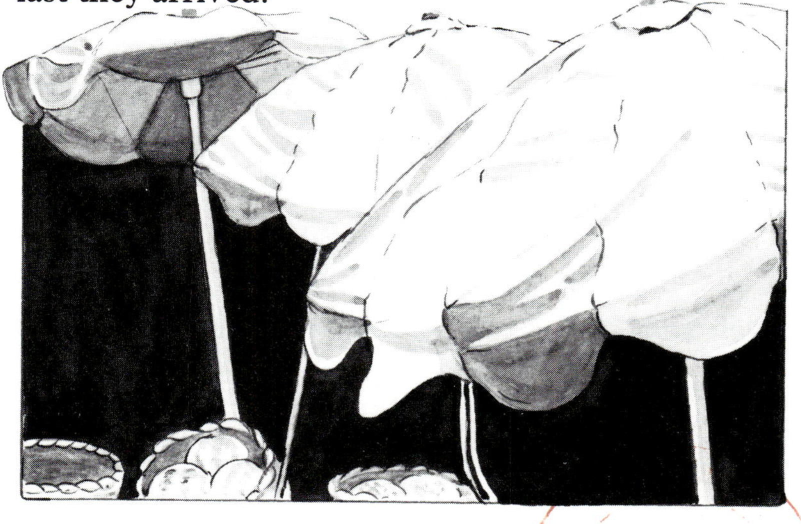

3

The Market

The market was littered with squashed pieces of fruit, papers twitching in the slight breeze, and, at places where sugar cane was sold, the long peelings of cane trash, sharp and crunchy underfoot. There were puddles left from the heavy rain of the night before, and a half swept-up pile of rubbish to be walked round with care.

In spite of the mess on the ground, Calvin enjoyed the market. He liked the bustle and the business, and he loved the fragrance of the ripe fruits as their scents blended together. He made his way through to the section where his mother always set up her goods, greeting several people he knew on the way. Miss May, who lived near his family in Ginger River, called out to him from her stall. She had a bruised mango she could not sell, and she deftly cut off the soft section. The rest she handed to Calvin, and he sank his teeth gratefully into the ripe flesh. Her pitch was a stall in the new market building where the best positions were. It was shady and cool, and dry when it rained. Those who sold in there got higher prices.

Calvin's mother was outside. She had to content

herself with a faded umbrella for shade, and her oranges were spread out on a piece of sacking on the ground. It was not a good spot, but her oranges were sweet and juicy, and she had regular customers. As Calvin arrived, she was serving someone with a dozen ortaniques. Their bright orange skins contrasted with the greener skins of the regular oranges.

'You very late,' she said to Calvin. 'Wh'appen then?'

Calvin explained briefly about the hospital visit, but she hardly listened. Another customer had come.

'Tek out the heggs,' she commanded, and Calvin started to unwrap them and arrange them in the wooden racks behind the oranges. 'Miss 'Ilda soon comin' back for some.'

'Stop 'ere for a while,' she said when he had finished. 'Mi soon comin' back.'

Calvin knew that 'soon comin' back' could mean an hour or more, but he liked looking after the stall. His mother vanished through the crowds, glad of a little time off to join in the market gossip.

Calvin sat on the upturned bucket his mother used, and waited. From time to time, people stopped and asked ''Ow much a dozen fi the horanges?' A few of them bought some, but most passed on to repeat the question at a dozen stalls before choosing which to buy.

Miss Hilda came and looked at him suspiciously.

'Where your mother garn?' she demanded.

'She soon come,' replied Calvin vaguely. 'She tell me to keep you some heggs.'

That wasn't exactly what she had said, but Calvin knew how to be tactful, and she beamed at him.

''Ow much?' she asked.

'Five daler seventy,' said Calvin promptly. Miss Hilda made a face, but she too had been round the stalls, and knew it was a fair price. Calvin wrapped her up a dozen, carefully using the same pieces of paper he had unwrapped them from a few minutes before, and placing them in a sturdy paper bag.

The fat lady from the bus came along, and started to feel the oranges.

'Marnin' Mrs Williams', said a passer-by. The fat lady returned the greeting with only the slightest of nods.

'Them sweet?' she asked, and Calvin nodded. If she recognised him, she gave no sign of it. When he had told her how much they were, she sniffed and went elsewhere. He was not sorry to see her go. She had not had a good word for anyone all day.

Two policemen strolled by, looking important in their blue trousers with red stripes down the side. There was nothing for them to worry about, and they were taking it easy in the market sunshine.

At last Calvin's mother came back, and Calvin gave her the money he had taken. She brought a purse out from the folds of her clothing and put it all in. Then she settled down on the bucket, legs akimbo, skirt pulled around her knees.

'Mr Jenkins sellin' 'is heggs at five daler ninety,' she remarked with satisfaction. 'Now, go and ask Miss May for some tea.'

She gave him two eggs to take to Miss May, who was brewing a cannikin of tea on a small spirit stove. In return, Miss May handed him a large mugful of tea, generously whitened with thick sweet condensed milk. He carried it to his mother, feeling a little thirsty himself, and she gave him twenty cents to buy a kisko-pop.

He could hear a long drawn out 'keees-ko, kees-ko-lay!' from the boy, who was selling them. The boy took Calvin's money and pulled out a long green ice pole from the thick layers of polythene in which he kept them cold. Calvin peeled down the wrapper and sucked it with enjoyment. It seemed like an ordinary market Saturday.

Suddenly Calvin noticed the girl in the beret who had left the bus at the same time as the rude boys. She was leaning against the entrance post of the main market building, chewing vigorously, and her shopping basket, filled with calaloo, was beside her. She stared ahead of her, looking as if she were interested in nothing in particular but, with a slight start, Calvin noticed one of the boys walking down

the concourse towards her. As the boy passed close beside her, she gave no sign that she recognised him.

Calvin upturned his kisko wrapper to empty the last of the now melted juice into his throat and wandered back to his mother's pitch. Remembering everything that had happened on the bus, he was sure that they were all up to no good. Still, there was nothing he could do about it.

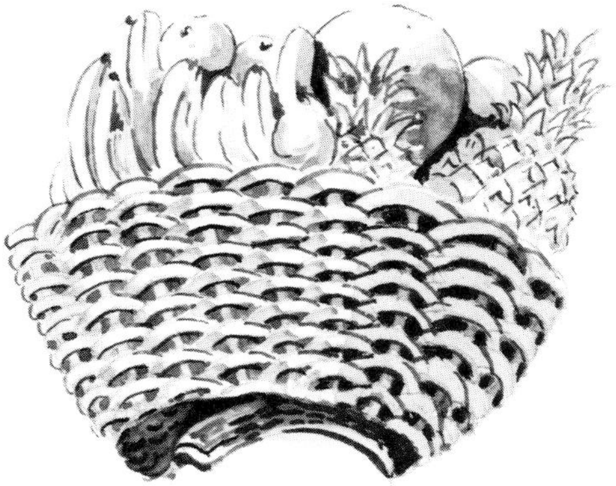

When he got back, an elderly lady called Miss Edie was buying oranges. She packed them into her basket and then felt for her purse. Suddenly her face crumpled with agitation. The purse wasn't there. 'Oh Lord, me purse garn!' she gasped. Miss Edie made a second frantic search through her basket, and then began to howl loudly.

'Me purse garn, me purse garn, someone tief me purse!' The noise brought a crowd of sympathetic onlookers. Her basket was searched several times more and so was the ground nearby. Still there was no sign of the purse.

The policemen arrived on the scene, a little sorry that their peaceful stroll had been interrupted. Hysterically, Miss Edie, explained what had happened.

'Is forty daler!' she wept. 'All me week's money garn!'

The policemen shrugged their shoulders. There were hundreds of people in the market – anyone might have it.

'You shouldn't keep it in de basket . . .' one of them began, but she silenced him with an angry exclamation. It was too late for that sort of advice.

Miss Edie's son came hurrying over. He wore shorts, a T-shirt, and a straw hat. He was muscular and strong, but as he approached Miss Edie, he was full of gentleness and concern.

'Wh'appen, Mamma?' he asked.

It all came out again. The surrounding crowd listened once more to the whole story. The man turned to the policeman.

'What you doin' 'bout it?' he demanded. The policemen shrugged their shoulders again. There was nothing they could do, but that didn't stop Miss Edie's son from shouting at them crossly.

Calvin thought he knew where the money was. He told his mother quietly about the pickpockets on the bus, and how he had just seen the girl, who, he was convinced, was part of the set-up.

His mother pursed her lips. It seemed a bit of a long-shot. Nevertheless, she called Miss Edie's son over, and Calvin told him the story again. 'Where is dis girl?' he asked, and Calvin pointed her out. She was still standing at the same spot, still looking vacantly about and still chewing.

'A'right,' he said, and strode off towards her. Calvin wondered what he would do, and almost wished he hadn't mentioned it. The crowd followed too, and so did the policemen.

The big man went straight to the point. 'How come you tief my mama's purse?' he said.

For just a second, the girl's jaws stopped moving. Then she began chewing again, and spoke coolly to the angry man.

'Mi no tief notten,' she said. 'Mi standing 'ere for 'alf an hour.' A higgler, weighing ackees on a spring balance for a customer, backed her up. 'That right, mister. She bin 'ere long time.'

'Mi no come over 'ere at all, Micky,' said Miss Edie, fearful that her son had gone too far. But he hadn't finished. He had seen something on the ground among the ackee skins the higgler had been peeling off. He reached down and picked it up.

'Is that your purse?' he asked, handing it to his mother.

It was. She eagerly clicked it open. Her face fell again when she found it was empty.

Micky turned to the girl again, and seized the basket from her. There was fear in her face now. One of the policemen stepped forward, and said 'You can't tek 'er basket, man.'

Micky threw off the restraining hand, and delved under the calaloo. In a moment he brought out a wad of money.

'Is my money!' said the girl, raising her voice for the first time. 'It mine!' said Miss Edie at the same moment, taking it from her son. 'You can' know it your money,' said the policeman. 'All money look the same you know.'

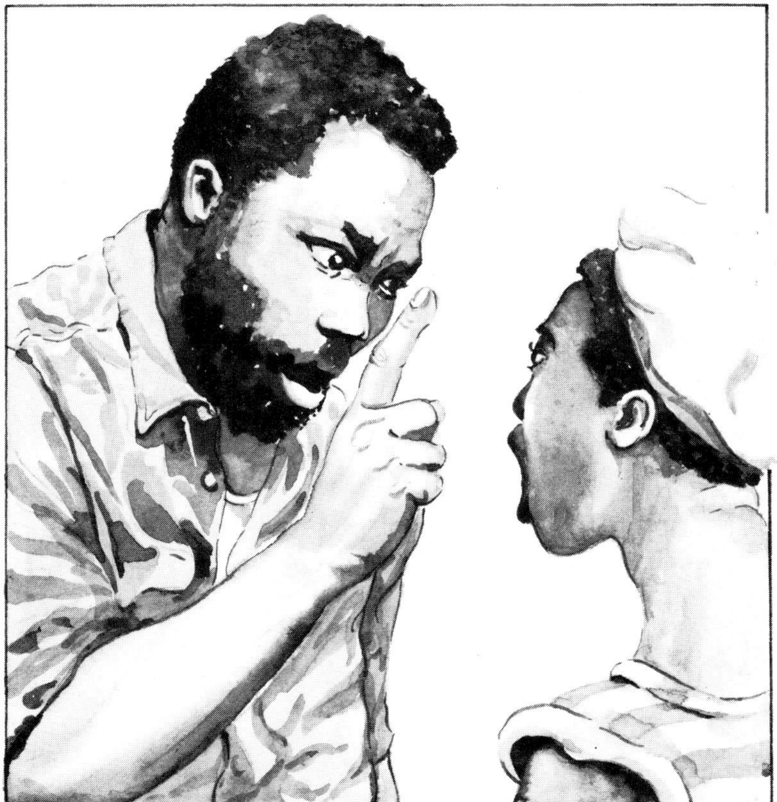

But Miss Edie took the folded wad of notes, and opened it. A tattered photograph fluttered out. She pounced on it triumphantly. 'I always carry a picture of Micky in me purse,' she said, and held it up for all to see. There was laughter in the crowd. Was this picture of a small boy, standing uncomfortably in a suit made for a special occasion, really her big, burly son?

The policemen moved up to the girl who glared at them defiantly as they led her away. The old lady happily counted up her money and put it back in her purse. The crowd began to break up.

Calvin's mother was anxious to return to her stall, left unattended for several minutes now.

'Hexcuse me,' she said. 'You never pay for the oranges, you know.'

And Miss Edie, a big smile covering her face, paid up.

4

Return Journey

King Fernando was on the way back up the hill at the end of the day.

Calvin was standing in his favourite spot, just behind the driver. In this position, he got a lot of heat from the engine but he didn't mind. He enjoyed watching Joe driving, and he liked to have the same view of the road ahead that Joe had. They were just turning into Redmount. He looked out at the wide gully, which carried rainwater down from the hillside villages. They went past a large cream painted church with trim gardens. The houses at Redmount were large and comfortable looking, with plenty of trees in their yards.

'One stop, Driver!' called several people.

When the bus pulled up, Chereme and her mother were among those getting off. They had been at the hospital all day. The little girl looked a lot happier than she had done in the morning. Her arm was tied up in a neat white sling and she was smiling now. She recognised Calvin and beamed at him. Joe saw them leaving and lifted a hand off the steering wheel for a moment.

Even when these people got out, there was no

spare space in the bus. Passengers were crammed three to a seat, with dozens more standing. Small shopping bags were pushed under seats, and on to the narrow luggage rack above people's heads. Bulkier packages were on the roofrack.

Calvin had enjoyed climbing up the spindly ladder to help with packing the roofrack at the start of the journey. His mother's unsold oranges and ortaniques were up there, packed away into a cardboard box. It was also loaded high with cabbages in sacks, crates of Red Stripe beer and Pepsi Cola, and great bunches of green bananas.

Calvin smiled to himself as he remembered the expression on fat Mrs Williams' face when the conductress had refused to let her take her bunch of bananas into the bus. Everybody else had uncomplainingly put their bulky items on the top, but it didn't suit her, so she grumbled. The bananas had gone up there anyway and she had clambered into the bus muttering 'How shall I know which are mine?'

When Calvin climbed down and got into the bus himself, he found her still fussing. Somehow she had got herself a seat near the front. Now she was trying to get the person next to her to move her bag over on the luggage rack overhead, and make room for her basket. It was plainly too large for the rack, but Mrs Williams insisted. In the end it was up there, wedged firmly by the bag next to it.

Joe didn't turn round, but Calvin glimpsed his eyes in the mirror watching all that was going on.

Leaving Redmount behind, the bus crossed the gully and climbed up the hill. It was a sleepy, sunny afternoon. A few goats were foraging among the bushes by the roadside. An old man sat on a grassy patch looking after a few creamy coloured cows. Sitting or leaning in doorways, the people watched King Fernando pass. At Ardgarten, the hillside on the left of the road was clustered with shacks. A few people got off there and disappeared up into the small houses.

A few moments after the bus started again, the conductress tapped Joe's shoulder and he stopped. She jumped out and ran round to the back to chase

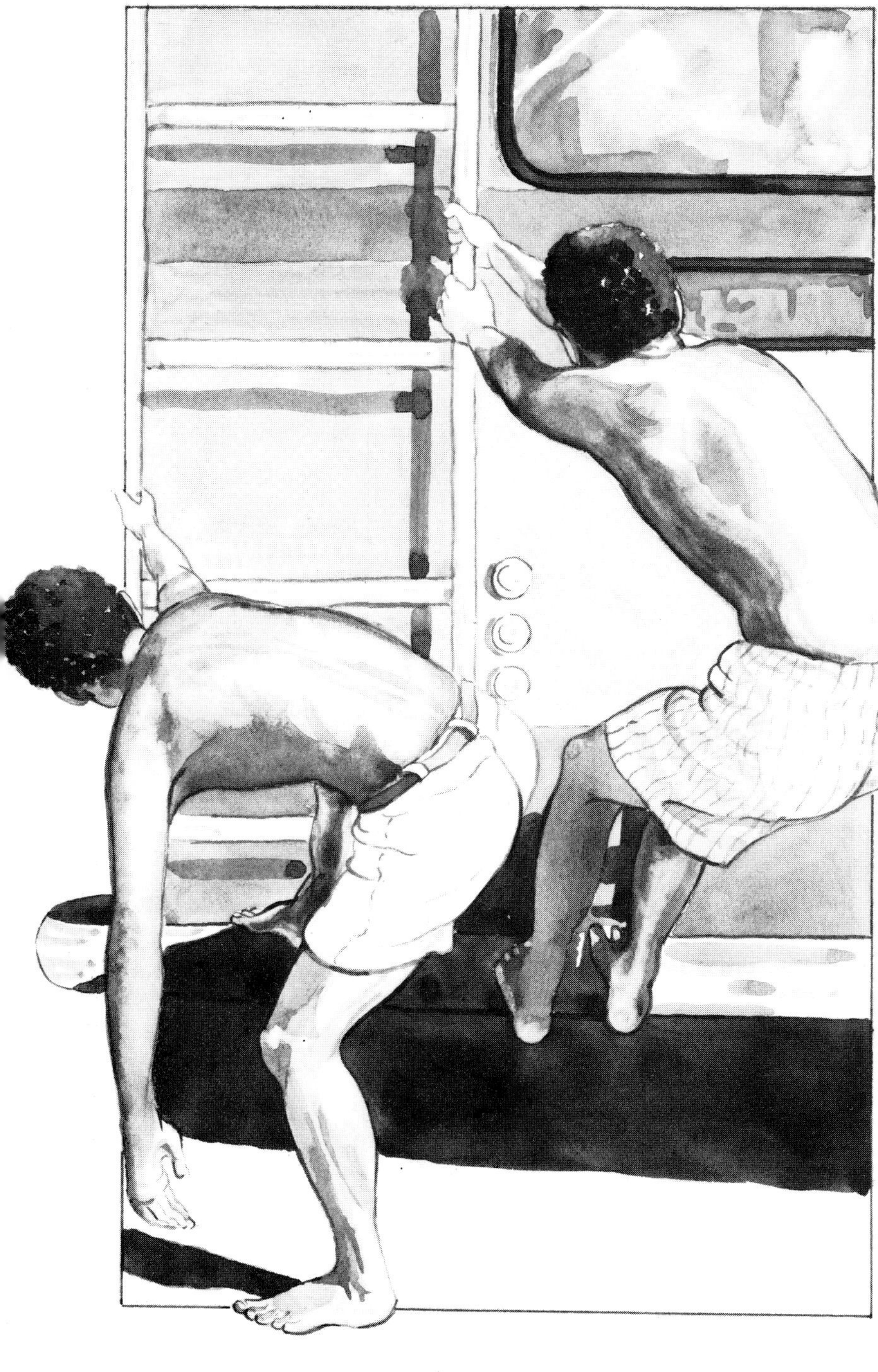

off three half-naked boys who had been standing on the rear bumper, clinging on for a free ride. They scattered, laughing, and vanished into Ardgarten.

The conductress got back on board, clicking her tongue with disapproval. Once, Calvin would have thought it fun himself to ride like that, but only a few days before his mother had shown him a report in the *Daily Gleaner*. It had described an accident where a boy hanging on the back of a bus had been swung off on a sharp bend, and run over by a car coming in the opposite direction. Even now he shuddered at the thought of it.

From here on, the climb became steeper. The road wound its way up the edge of the mountain, twisting and turning to take the easiest route. There were just as many houses here. To the right of the road, gateways led down flights of steps and little could be seen of the houses except their corrugated roofs. To the left of the road, however, the houses were built on the upward slope. Their fronts were supported on long stilts, while the backs rested on the ground. Calvin's mother sometimes remarked that if there were a breeze, they would all blow away. But the wind often blew, and they were still there.

This was Limegrove, and quite a few people got off. There was room now for most people to sit, although Calvin was happy where he was, and remained standing.

The person next to Mrs Williams got off here. Before anyone else could sit beside her, Mrs Williams quickly spread herself across the seat. Calvin noticed that the bag which had been wedged in her basket had been removed. The basket itself now looked very unsteady. He leaned over, and tapped Mrs Williams on the shoulder.

'Hexcuse me, Mrs . . .' he began.

She glared at him. Her eyes were little, and her face puffy.

''Scuse me Miss . . .' Calvin tried again. That basket would soon fall.

'Shut your noise, lickle boy,' said Mrs Williams rudely, and turned away from him, settling herself more comfortably on to the double seat.

Calvin shrugged his shoulders. He returned his

attention to watching the road ahead. For a second he noticed Joe's eyes in the mirror again, and realised that Joe, although he never said much, watched everything that was going on in the bus.

The engine squealed up a particularly steep part of the road. Coming to a flatter bit, Joe changed gear, and, as always, the bus jerked as he let the clutch in.

The jerk was all the basket needed. Gently it toppled over. Calaloo floated down like leaves off a tree. A bag of eggs, which Mrs Williams had packed near the top, fell on her lap; it was the first she knew of what was happening. She jumped to her feet to save the basket, the bag of eggs falling the rest of the way to the floor as she did so. She was already too late. Everything was dropping. Tomatoes, cho-cho, oranges, a large piece of yam, an Ugli, and a pound of sweet potatoes rained down on her, and finally the basket itself bounced off her outstretched arm, and clattered to the floor. There was a gale of laughter from the passengers behind, who had had a grandstand view of what was happening.

The bus slammed to a stop. The jolt set everything rolling again, and several tomatoes got trodden on. From the egg bag at Mrs Williams' feet, an unspeakable mess was spreading.

Joe stepped out of his seat, and stood looking down the bus. A silence fell. Joe never did this sort

of thing. Everybody in the bus wondered what would happen next.

Without a word, he looked at the mess. He looked at Mrs Williams. He got out of the bus, walked round to the storage compartment at the back. In a moment he returned, carrying a bucket and rag which he handed to Mrs Williams.

Meekly, she mopped up the worst of the mess. While she was doing it, one or two of the other passengers collected her undamaged items and packed them back into the basket for her. Joe just stood and watched.

When she had finished, she sat back on the seat, with her basket beside her. But Joe had not quite finished with her.

He looked at the basket and said, 'If you want two seat, you should pay two fare.' She snatched the basket onto her lap, and pressed herself far enough over to leave one seat vacant. No one came and sat on it.

Joe started the bus off again. For a second, he caught Calvin's eye in the mirror. Calvin wasn't sure, but he thought he saw a faint wink.

The climb was nearly over now. The bus was coming to Taylor's Hill. In a moment, they would reach Calvin's favourite part of the whole journey. Coming round a last bend, there would suddenly be a wonderful view of the city spread out below, the sea beyond, glimmering blue, and the distant mountains on the other side of the bay. At this point, nothing stood between the bus and the view. The edge of the steep drop was marked only by a flimsy wooden fence on the right of the road.

As the bus came into the bend, Calvin craned forward to enjoy the view.

Down the hill, a car came hurtling. The driver could not have heard King Fernando's horn, and was going much, much too fast. He was cutting the corner on their side of the road.

One moment there was just the view. The next, Joe, with a startled curse, was flinging the bus over to the right and stamping on the brakes in an effort to avoid the car.

The bus skidded across the road. There was a sickening lurch and a sound of tearing metal as the car crashed into the back of it.

Calvin felt a shriek rising inside him as he saw the fence burst into pieces, and the front of the bus slide off the edge of the clifftop into nothingness.

5

Rescue Operation

Calvin was in a state of hopeless terror as he felt the front of the bus dip beneath him. He saw the whole view tilting upwards for a long, long second. Then some instinct made him fling himself to the floor, and grab hold of the nearest solid object – the base of a seat. He closed his eyes, and waited for the awful plunge. The bus was full of screaming and shouting.

The plunge didn't come. The screams tailed away into a ragged sort of silence, and Calvin opened his eyes again. He could see nothing from on the floor, and carefully he scrambled to his feet again, wondering. All around him, other passengers were sitting, dazed, fearful, blinking, and – for the moment – silent.

He thought to himself, perhaps this is what it is like to be dead.

He hardly dared to look out of the window, but, when he did he saw that nothing had changed. They were still poised above the drop, with the view gently swaying up and down. Calvin realised that the bus had halted on the very edge, balanced like a giant see-saw.

'Hey, we not fallin'.'

'Wh'appen?'

'You a'right, Mamma?'

'The bus stick 'ere.'

'Come on, let's get out.'

The first reaction as the passengers realised they were alive was to get out through the door, and there was a sudden surge of movement towards it. The bus started to rock dangerously.

'STOP! Sit down!' It was the voice of Micky, Miss Edie's son, who was ably taking command of the situation.

'You step out of dat door, and you'll fly, man,' he said. The door, being at the front of the bus, was poised over empty space.

'An' if you all run down the front, you'll tip the 'ole bus over,' he continued. His words, and the lurches of the bus, convinced everybody and the forward rush was halted.

'Now, stay still. We 'ave to t'ink what to do.'

A few people eased back into their places, and the bus stopped swaying. Loud chatter broke out, and there was some crying.

'Anyone 'urt?' demanded Micky.

'Joe's 'urt,' said the conductress. The driver was leaning onto the steering wheel, groaning a bit. She was with him.

'Dere a lady back 'ere 'urt,' came another voice. At the very back of the bus, where the car had hit it, glass had cascaded onto one of the passengers, who was badly cut.

'Anyone else?' asked Micky, but apart from a few bruises, everybody else in the bus was all right.

'Joe bang 'im chest on the steering wheel,' said the conductress.

'Tek 'im back and lay 'im on a seat,' Micky said. Joe, leaning heavily on the conductress, walked painfully back along the bus, and lay down gratefully on a seat which was cleared for him.

''Im ribs mash up,' remarked Micky.

At the back, a few people were helping the injured lady. Most of the passengers, however, were thinking only of getting out of the bus.

The obvious way out was through a window onto the solid ground at the back. There was a window there that had no glass in it, and the lady who had been sitting by it was pushing her children out. She passed down her basket, and clambered down herself. It was difficult, and there was a lot of grunting and heaving, but, after a bit, she was safely outside. Other people nearby followed her example. Before long, a dozen or more passengers had escaped this way, and the others were eagerly awaiting their turn.

But this escape brought new danger. The back, gradually becoming lighter than the front, suddenly rose into the air as the bus see-sawed once again on the brink of the cliff. A man who was half-way out through the window let go, and dropped to the ground – much further than he had expected to. He lay there winded. Inside the bus, screams and new cries of alarm began.

By now, quite a crowd had gathered. Several helpers had dragged the car driver from his vehicle. The car itself was hooked onto the bus in a mass of bent metal. It was probably this extra weight which had stopped the bus from plummetting over the cliff in the first place. The onlookers now stood looking helplessly at the back of the bus, which was two metres off the ground, with the remains of the car dangling from it.

Inside, Micky was directing operations again. He wanted to transfer more weight to the rear.

'Genckly, now,' he instructed. 'Walk back, walk back genckly.'

Everybody in the front eased their way backwards. After a while, to their relief, they felt the back go down again. At first it tipped slowly, but by the time the back wheels hit the ground, it was dropping quite fast.

The impact dislodged the car. At once, the front, no longer counterbalanced by that weight, went down again. There were more cries of despair, and despair changed to fear as a new movement began. The bus gently started to slide forward. It only went a little way, but everybody inside it knew that it only had to go a little further and it would be right over the edge.

The people outside had brought a rope. A man had gone underneath, and was tying it to the back axle. Dozens of people got hold of the rope and heaved, but they were unable to budge the bus. In the end, they gave up and the other end was fastened to a tree. It was something, but everyone knew that it wasn't nearly strong enough to hold the bus if it slid any further.

By now, all the passengers were as far back as they could go, but the bus was not going to see-saw again. The weight of the engine at the front was too great to be counterbalanced.

'OK,' said Micky, 'Out dat window again.'

A few more passengers climbed out, but it was difficult, with quite a long drop again outside. Calvin couldn't see how the two injured people could go out that way, for a start. There were several others, Mrs Williams for one, and Micky's mother, Miss Edie for another, who were hanging back. On the one hand they were eager to escape from the bus; on the other, they were reluctant – maybe not able – to clamber through the window and drop to the ground.

Suddenly he had an idea. He remembered how he had looked through a gap in the floor at the road rushing past beneath his feet.

King Fernando was about forty-five years old. In the time when it was built, the floor was made not of metal but by screwing wooden boards on to the chassis. These boards could be prised up to make an easy way out.

'Micky.' He tugged at the big man's shirt. Micky was trying, with some difficulty, to persuade Calvin's mother to go out through the window. He looked down impatiently, but his eyes gleamed when Calvin explained his plan. The two of them bent down and started trying to tear at the floorboards with their fingers in the widest parts of the cracks. The floorboards didn't budge.

'Need a bar,' grunted Micky.

Joe, still lying on a seat, his face screwed up with pain, pointed down the bus. Under the driver's seat was the starting handle.

'Use that,' he said.

'Can't go down the front, the bus tip over,' replied Micky.

'Me go. Me lickle an' light,' said Calvin, and then wished he hadn't.

'Wait a bit,' said Micky. He motioned all the other passengers even further back than they already were, and then said to Calvin 'Now – tek it easy.'

Calvin slowly moved down the bus. He stepped gently, trying to make himself light as he went. Through the windows, he could see the long fall on either side. The cliffside was studded with boulders. Calvin could imagine the bus bouncing from rock to rock as it fell. Here and there, stunted trees struggled for existence in thin pockets of soil. He thought, if it falls, I can jump out of the door and grab a tree. Then he put the thought from his mind. He knew perfectly well that if the bus fell, that would be the end for all of them.

He had reached the front. He grabbed the handle and made his way back as fast as he dared. Micky seized it from him, shoved it into a crack between floorboards and quickly levered up one, two, three boards. The ground was just below them.

Gently, Joe and the injured lady were passed down to the waiting hands of helpers outside. Mrs Williams was helped through. One by one, the other passengers lowered themselves down. Last of all came the conductress, and then Micky. They were all safe.

On the firm ground, they sat. Many passengers, the tension past, were weeping with relief. The nurse from the local health centre had arrived, and busied herself with the two injured people.

A wrecker's lorry came up the road, and attached its hook to the now abandoned bus. Its engine roared as it inched forward, and with loud scraping sounds the bus was gradually hauled back from the edge.

'Get mi basket,' Calvin's mother said to him, and he went into the bus and fetched it. It was hard to believe the horror of a few short minutes before. Calvin had a feeling that in a week or two, King Fernando would be patched up, and back on the run again.

'Come on,' his mother said to him. 'We 'ave to walk 'ome, don't we?'

Glossary of Words and Phrases

Ackees	A fruit with white flesh. It is cooked with saltfish to make a popular Jamaican dish.
Borin' in	Pushing in (a queue).
Calaloo	A green vegetable with a flavour similar to spinach.
Cane trash	Peelings from sugar cane.
'Cho!'	An exclamation of annoyance.
Cho cho	A vegetable similar to baby marrow, but with a stone in the middle.
Gleaner paper	Old newspaper. (*The Daily Gleaner* is Jamaica's main newspaper.)
Gully	A wide ditch for rain water.
Higgler	Street pedlar.
Kisko pop	An ice pole.
Mash up	Break.
'One stop driver'	Please stop here, I want to get off.
Pickneys	Children.
Sweet potatoes	Look like potatoes, but taste sweet. Used to make pudding.
Tief	Steal.
Wrecker's lorry	Breakdown truck.
Yam	A root vegetable.